P9-BBQ-379

Wildlife Preserves

Gift of Nathan Lyons
(1930–2016)

Other Books in The Far Side Series

The Far Side
Beyond The Far Side
In Search of The Far Side
Bride of The Far Side
Valley of The Far Side
It Came From The Far Side
Hound of The Far Side
The Far Side Observer
Night of the Crash-Test Dummies

Anthologies

The Far Side Gallery
The Far Side Gallery 2
The Far Side Gallery 3

Wildlife Preserves

A Far Side Collection

by Gary Larson

Andrews and McMeel
A Universal Press Syndicate Company
Kansas City • New York

The Far Side is syndicated internationally by Universal Press Syndicate.

Wildlife Preserves copyright © 1989 Universal Press Syndicate. All rights reserved. Printed in the United States of America. No part of this book may be used or reproduced in any manner whatsoever without written permission except in the case of reprints in the context of reviews. For information write Andrews and McMeel, a Universal Press Syndicate Company, 4900 Main Street, Kansas City, Missouri 64112.

ISBN: 0-8362-1842-6
Library of Congress Catalog Card Number: 88-83867

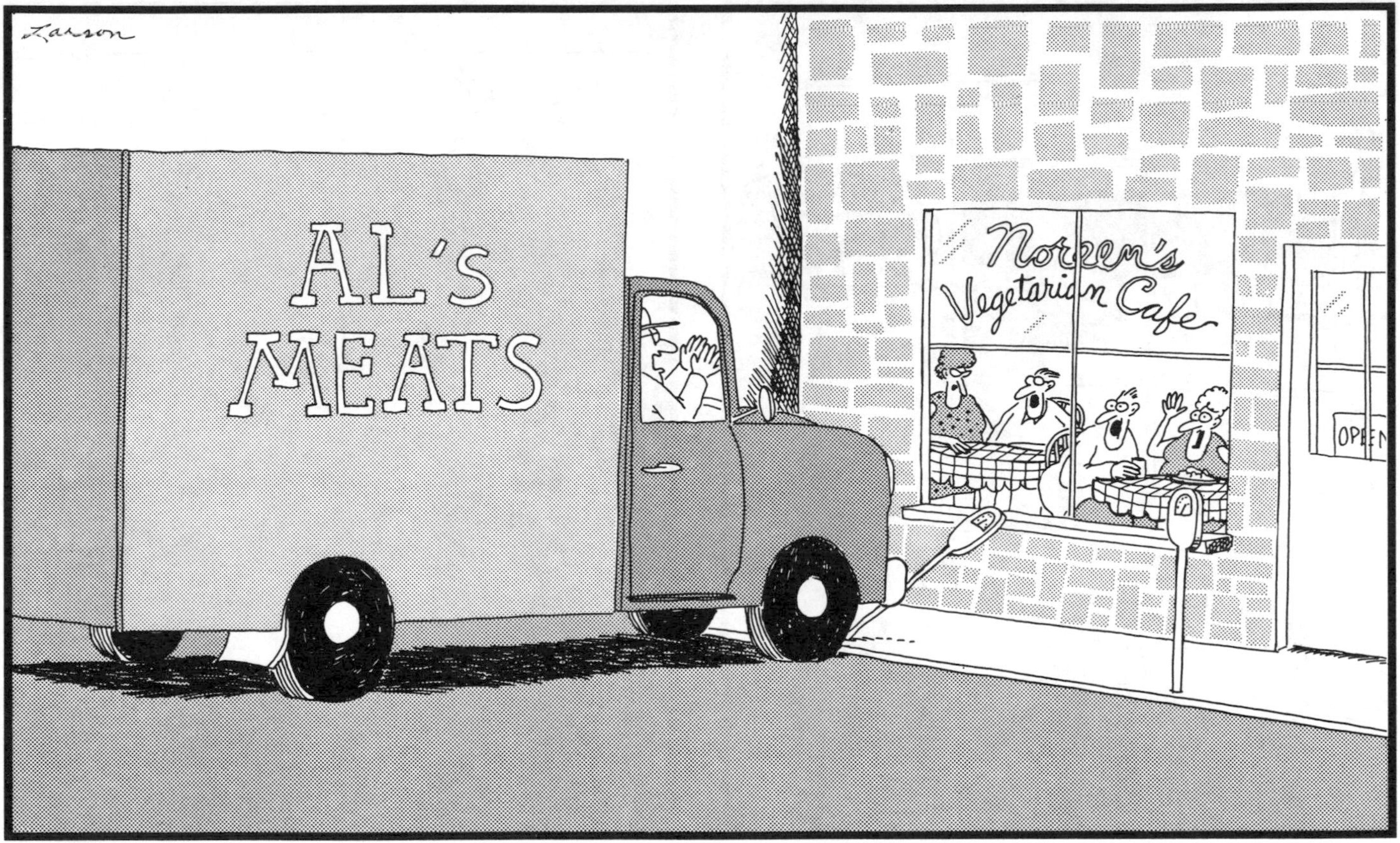
Larson
AL'S
MEATS
Noreen's
Vegetarian Cafe
OPEN

Life in the primordial soup

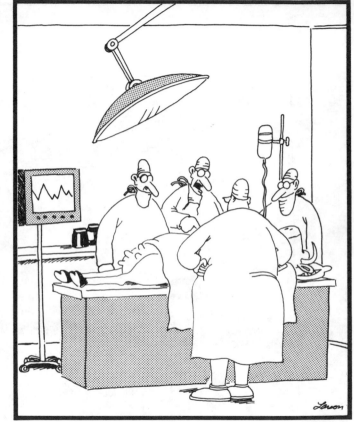

"Well, we've done everything we can; now we can only wait and see if she pulls through. ... If she doesn't, however, I got dibs on these ribs right here."

Karl Malden in his basement

Cowmen Miranda

Moses as a kid

"So then I says to Borg, 'You know, as long as we're under siege, one of us oughta moon these Saxon dogs.'"

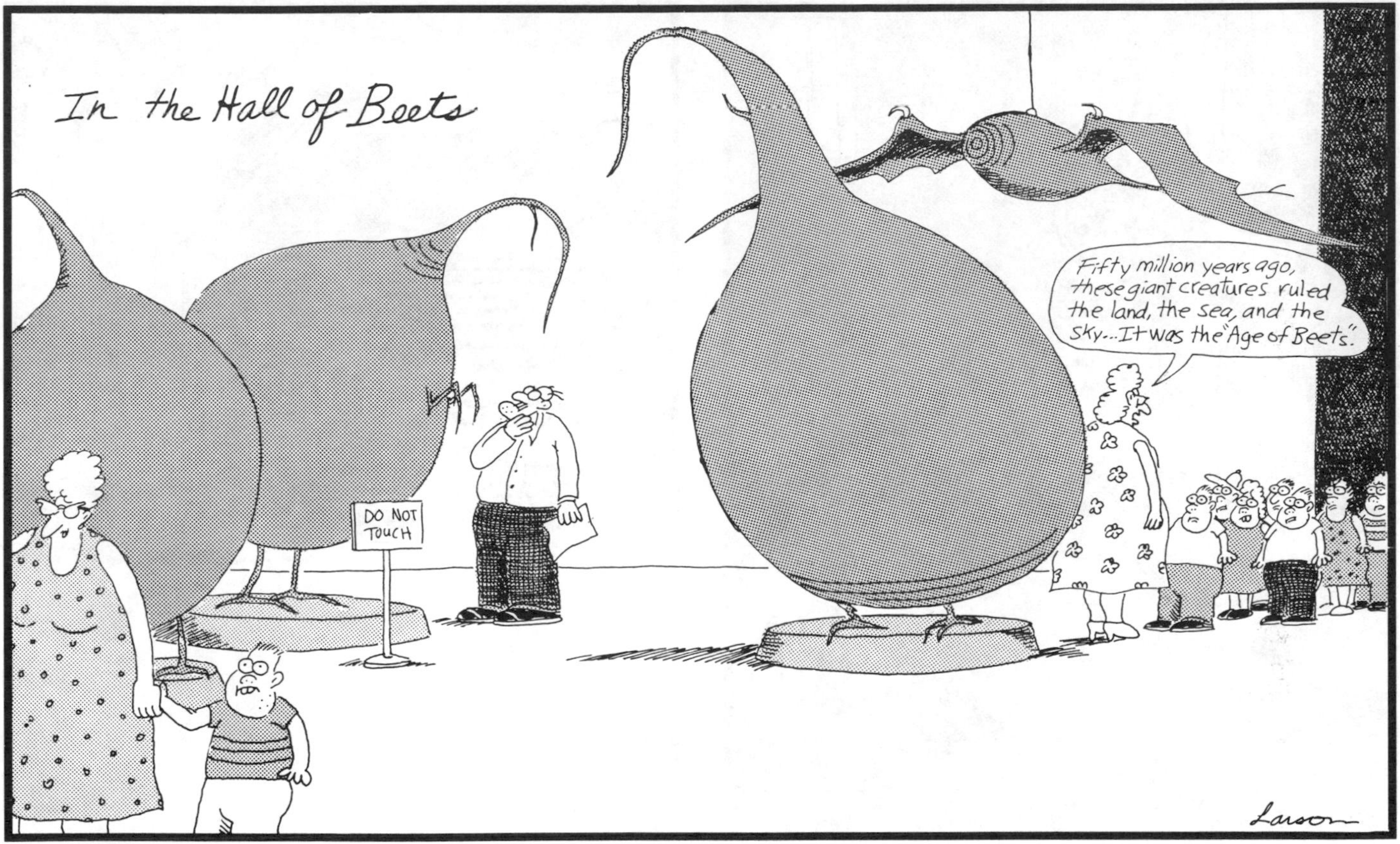
In the Hall of Beets
DO NOT TOUCH
Fifty million years ago, these giant creatures ruled the land, the sea, and the sky... It was the "Age of Beets."
Larson

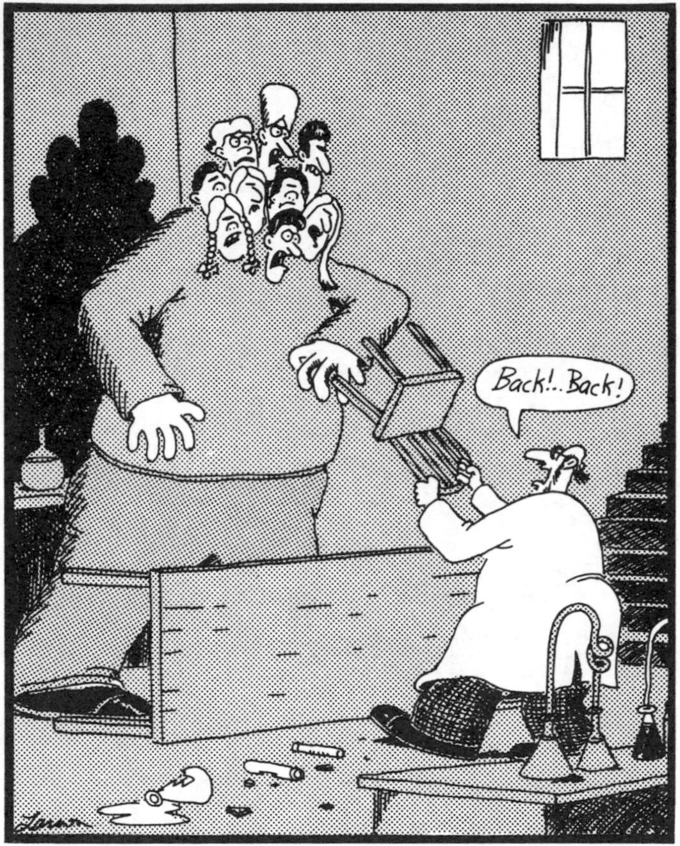
Back!..Back!

Suddenly, Dr. Morrissey's own creation, a hideous creature nine feet tall and bearing the heads of the Brady Bunch, turns against him.

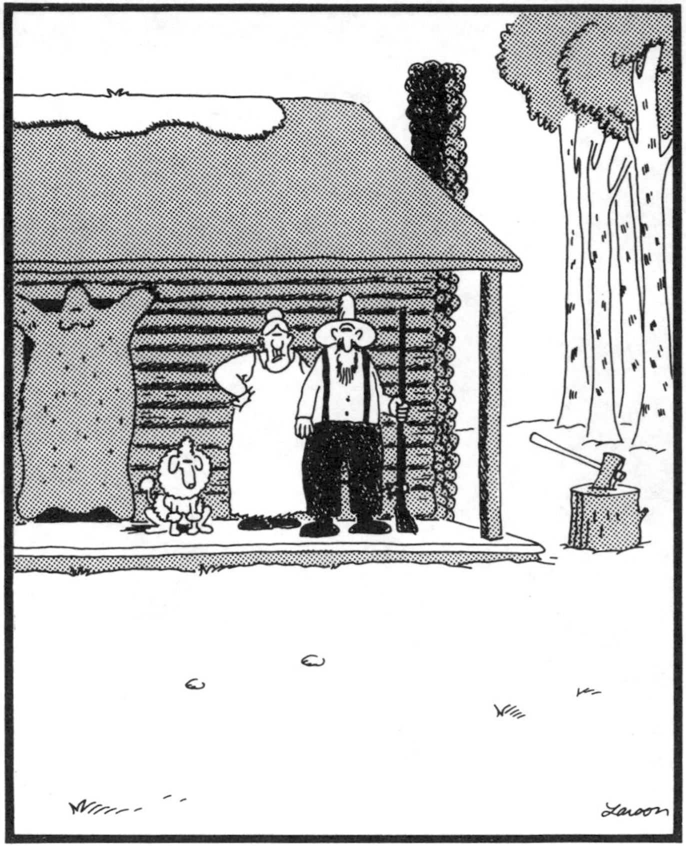

Early settlers of Beverly Hills

Slowly he would cruise the neighborhood, waiting for that
occasional careless child who confused him
with another vendor.

Construction birds at lunch

More Facts of Nature: As part of nature's way to help spread
the species throughout their ecological niche, bison often
utilize a behavior naturalists have described as "ballooning."

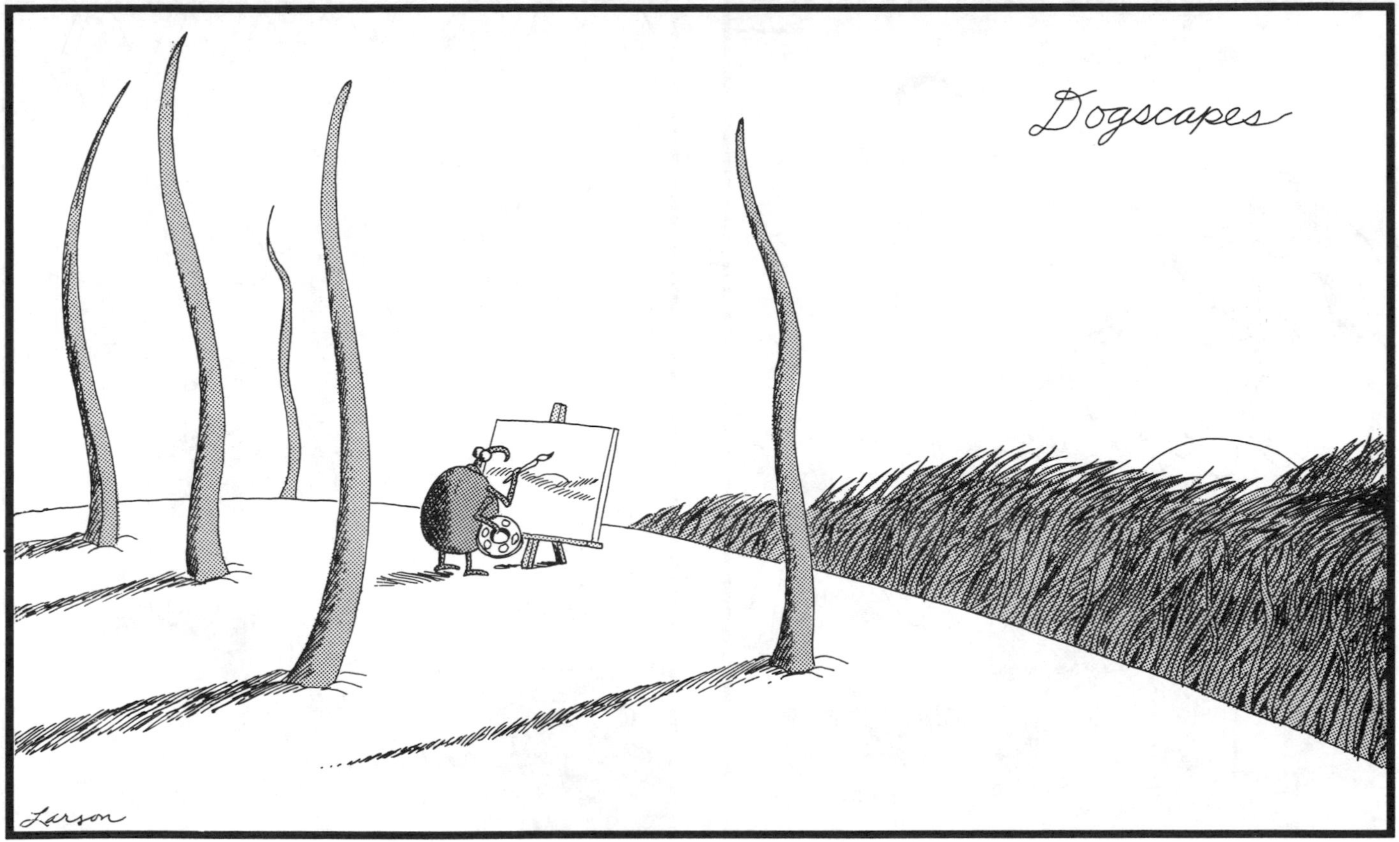
Dogscapes
Larson

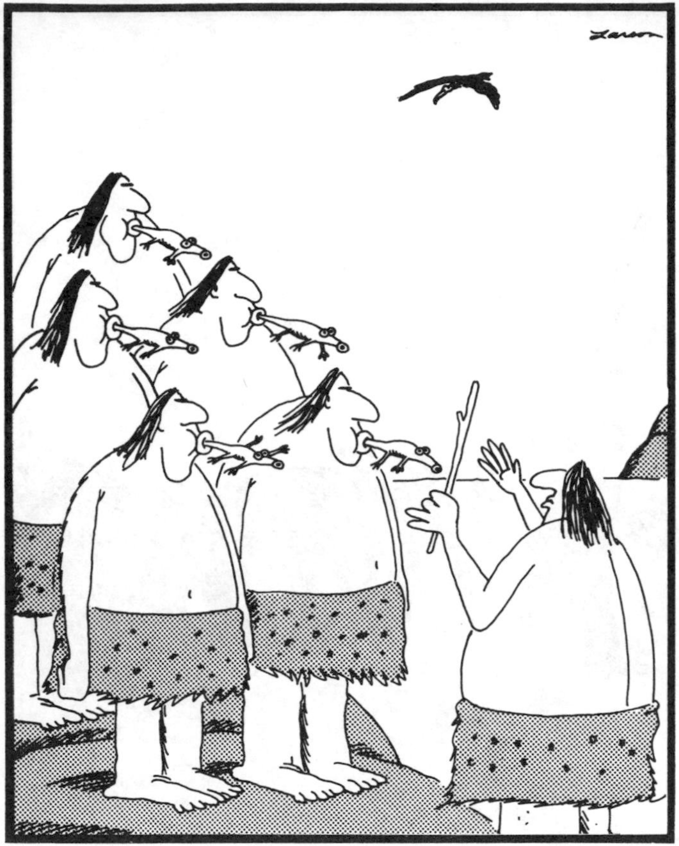

Early kazoo bands

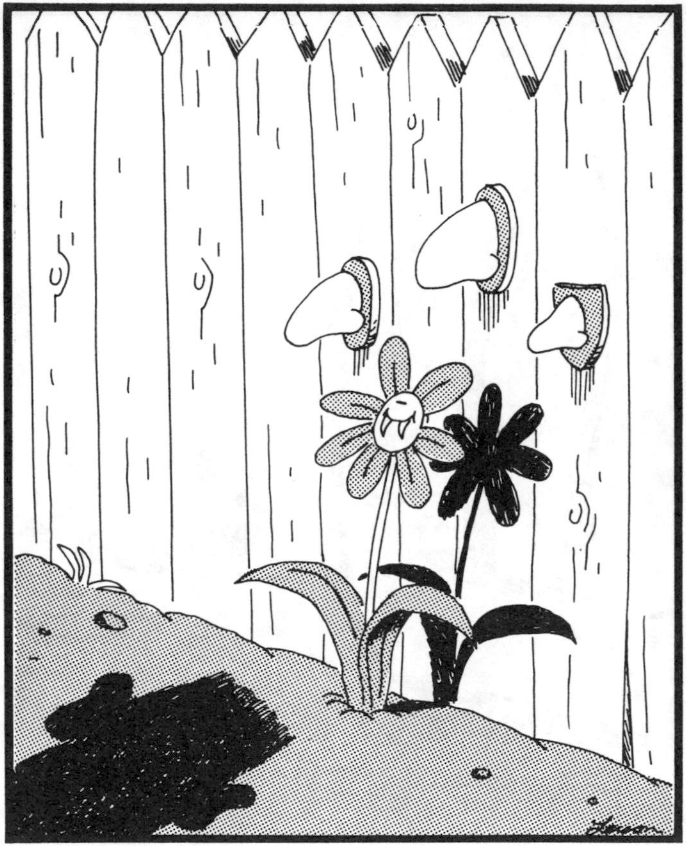

Anatidaephobia: The fear that somewhere, somehow, a duck is watching you.

Tethercat

"Just look at this room — body segments everywhere!"

The matador's nightmare

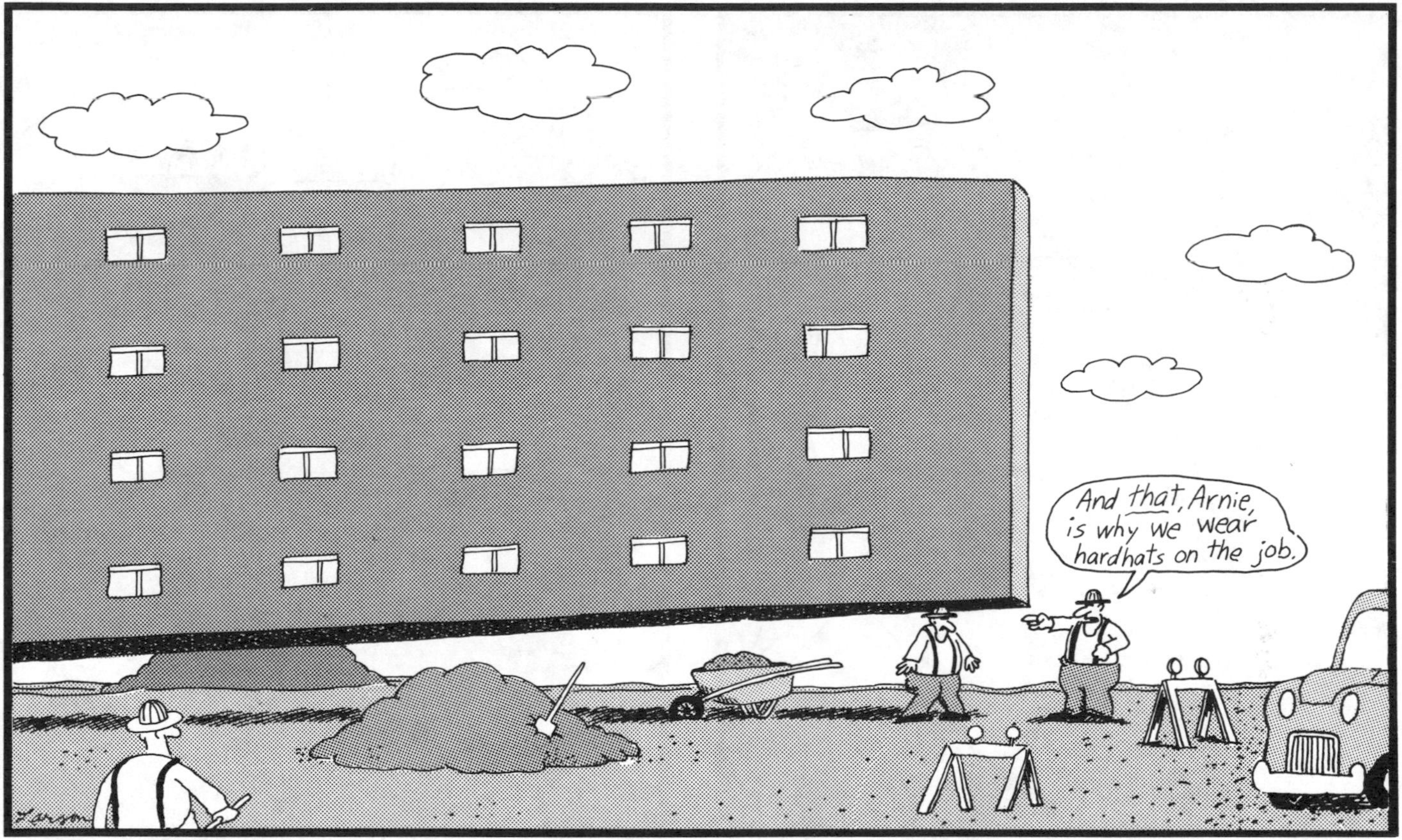
And that, Arnie, is why we wear hardhats on the job.
Larson

Primitive fraternities

"I don't know if this is such a wise thing to do, George."

"You know, Vern...the thought of what this place is gonna look like in about a week just gives me the creeps."

"Yo! Everyone down there! This is the jackal! I'm tired of slinking around in the shadows! ... I'm coming down to the kill! Is that gonna be cool with everyone! ... I don't want trouble!"

"Careful, Lyle! ... There's some cattle dancing!"

20

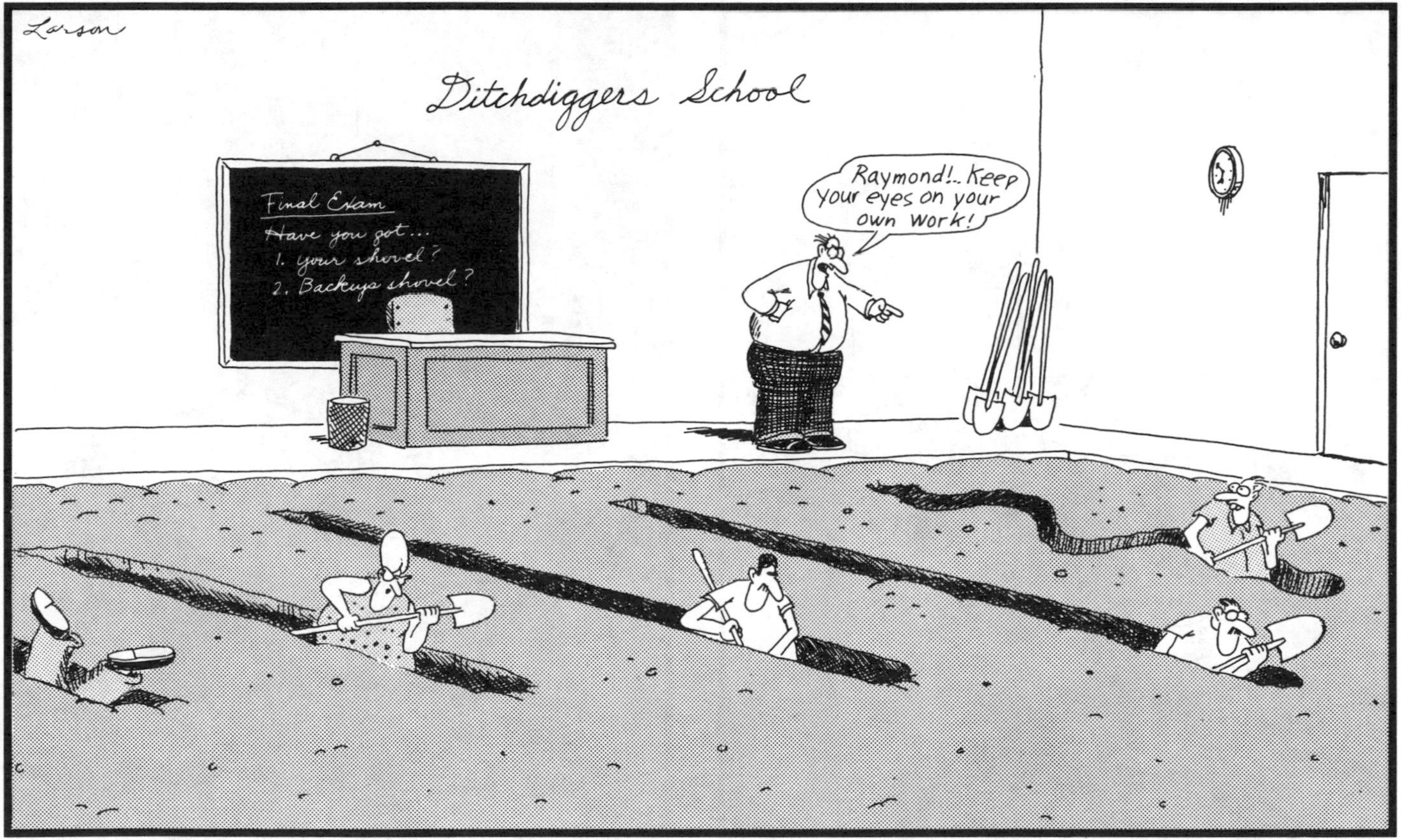
Larson
Ditchdiggers School
Final Exam
Have you got...
1. your shovel?
2. Backup shovel?
Raymond!.. Keep your eyes on your own work!

"Did you detect something a little ominous in the way they said, 'See you later'?"

"I tell you I've *had* it! …I'm not climbing into that getup one more time until you tell me why I'm always the *back* end!"

22

"Drive, Ted! We've stumbled into some cowtown."

"*Sure* it's true! ... Cross my heart and hope to die, stick a sharp chunk of obsidian in my eye."

The Potatoheads in Brazil

24

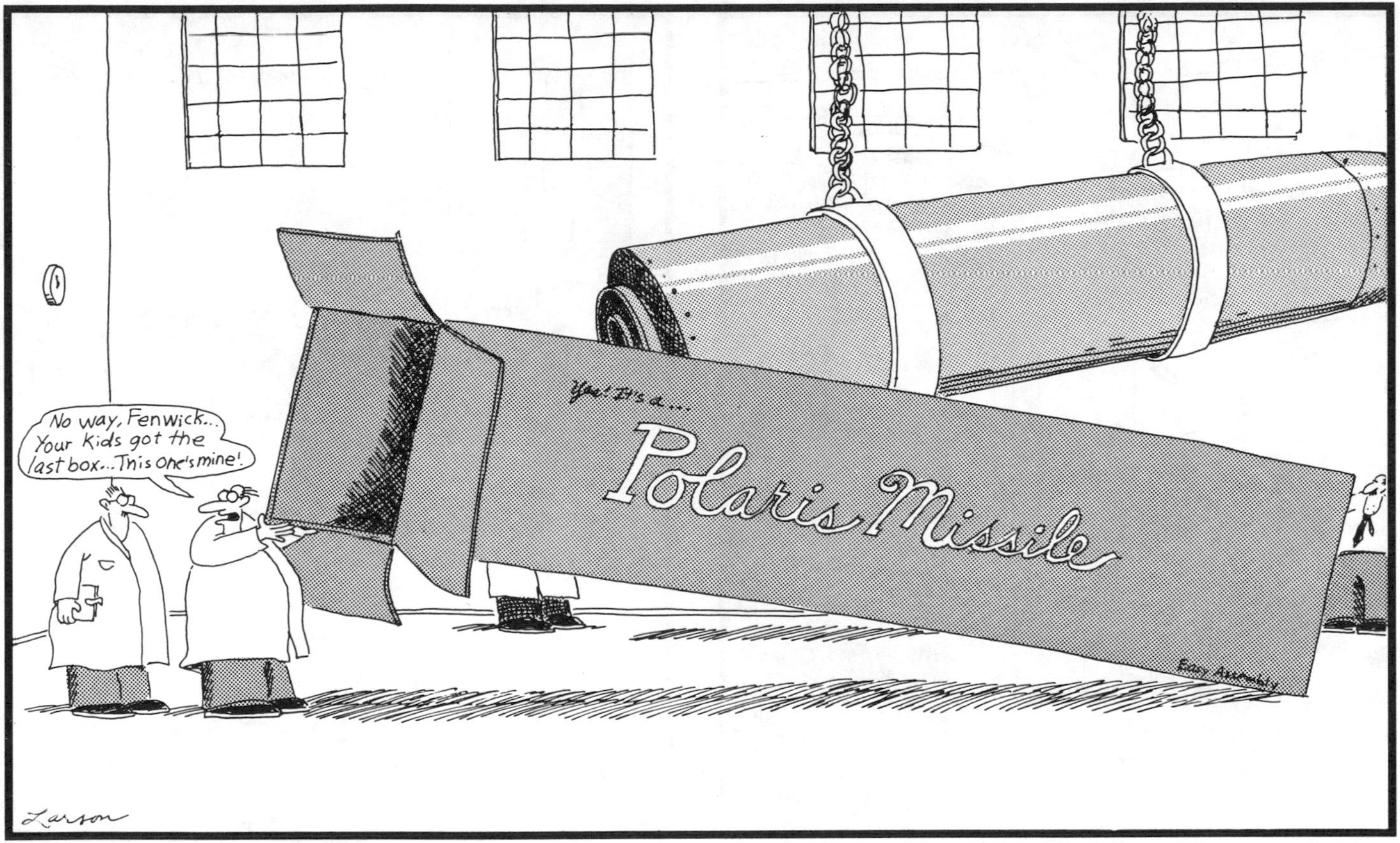
No way, Fenwick... Your kids got the last box... This one's mine!
Yes! It's a . . .
Polaris Missile
Easy Assembly
Larson

Bombardier beetles at home

"We understand your concern, ma'am — but this just isn't enough for us to go on. Now, you find the *other* half of your husband, and then we've got a case."

Mobile hobbyists

How the human egg is often deceived.

Frog pioneers

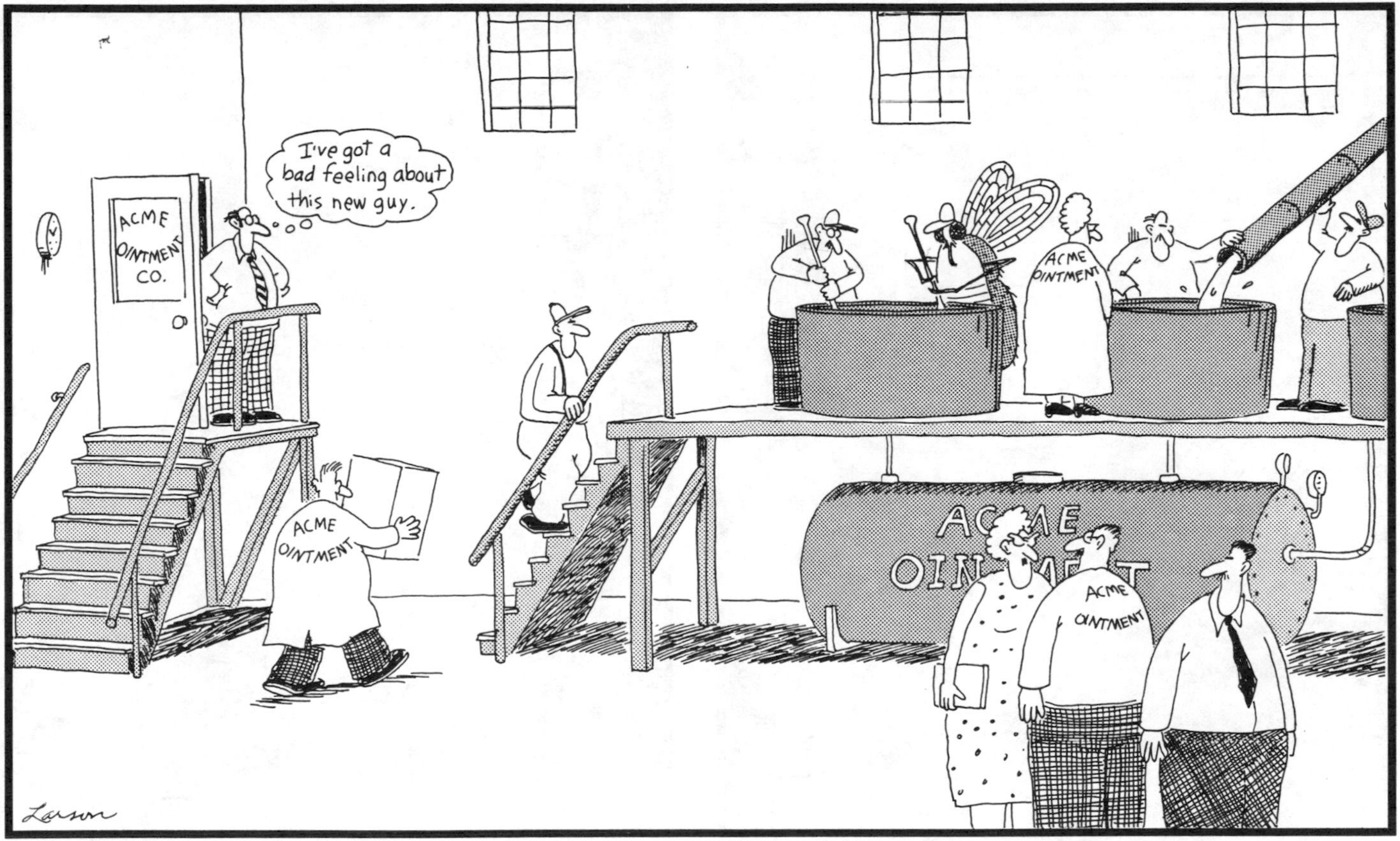
I've got a bad feeling about this new guy.
ACME OINTMENT CO.
ACME OINTMENT
ACME OINTMENT
ACME OINTMENT
Larson

"Aha! The murderer's footprints!
'Course, we all leave tracks like this."

"Hey! Ernie Wagner! I haven't seen you in, what's it been — 20 years? And hey — you've still got that thing growin' outta your head that looks like a Buick!"

"Good heavens, Bernie! We've got company! ...
And you're never going to catch that stupid squirrel anyway!"

On a clear day, Eugene rose and looked around him and,
regrettably, saw who he was.

Headhunter hutwarming

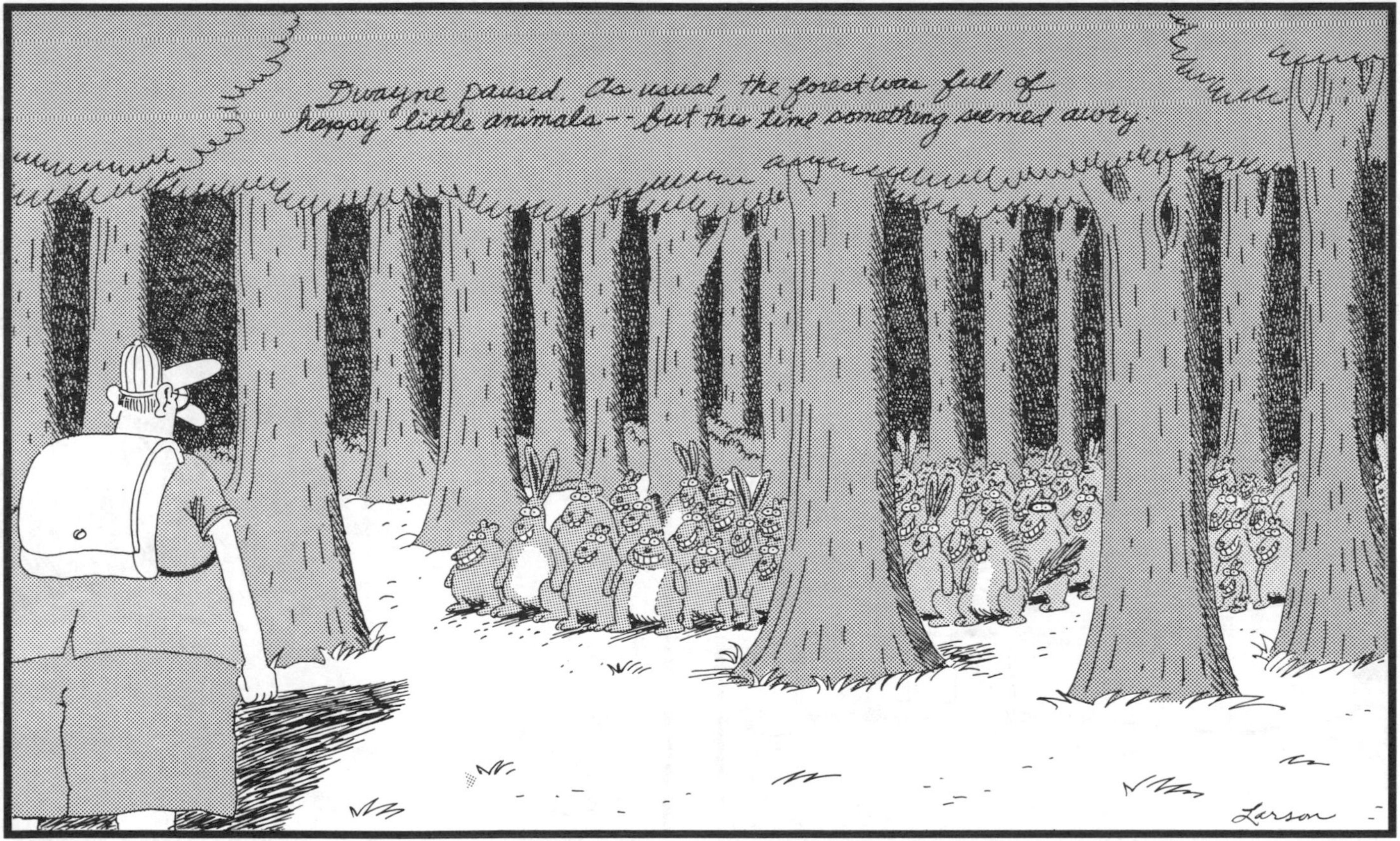
Dwayne paused. As usual, the forest was full of happy little animals -- but this time something seemed awry.
Larson

"Oh, good heavens, no, Gladys — not for me. ... I ate my young just an hour ago."

Nonunion wagon masters

34

"Ooooooweeeeee! This thing's been here a looooooooong time. Well, thank God for ketchup."

"OK, when I say 'draw,' we draw. ... Ready? ... One, two, three — STRAW! ... OK, just checkin' your ears. ... One, two, three — CLAW! ... OK, DRAWbridge! ... "

Vinci Bros.
Cockroach Farm

"Hours of revolting entertainment!"

"Now remember, Cory, show us that you can take good care of these little fellows and maybe *next* year we'll get you that puppy."

Splattered with juice and hooting excitedly, Neanderthals are depicted here as they proceed to carve up their favorite kill, the woolly watermelon.

Hell's Cafeteria

Scene from *Return of the Nose of Dr. Verlucci*

38

Why people named Buddy hate to drive

"What? You're just going to throw the tail away? ... Why, in *my* day, we used every goldang *part* of a mammoth!"

The Fullertons demonstrate Sidney's trick knee.

Sucker fish at home

As the cactus stood watch over the sun-drenched land, a red-tailed hawk hung motionless in the desert sky. Little stirred, except an occasional lizard scurrying for shade or a tumblenerd drifting by.

"Why, thank you. ... Thank you very much!"

"I can't believe it! This is impossible! Nothing here but — wait!
Wait! I see something! ... Yes! There they are — granola bars!"

"Hold it right there, young lady! Before you go out, you take off some of that makeup and wash off that gallon of pheromones!"

Street physicians

Embedded in Styrofoam "shoes," Carl is sent to "sleep with the humans."

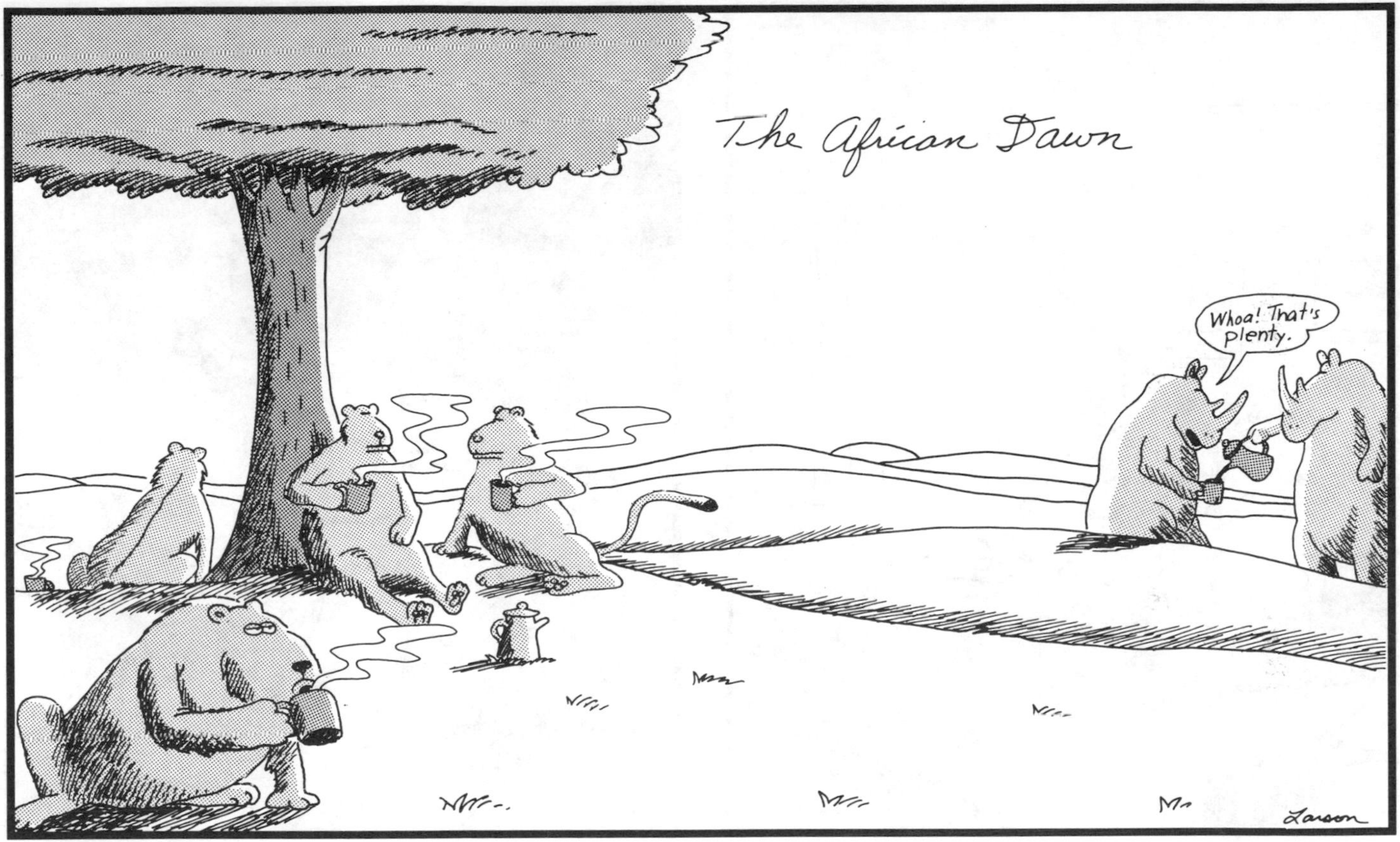
The African Dawn
Whoa! That's plenty.
Larson

"I built the forms around him just yesterday afternoon when he fell asleep, and by early evening I was able to mix and pour."

"Pretty cool, Dewey. ... Hey! Shake the jar and see if they'll fight!"

46

"Mr. Cummings? This is Frank Dunham in Production. ... We've got some problems. Machine No. 5 has jammed, several of the larger spools have gone off track, the generator's blown, and, well, everything seems to be you-know-what."

Infamous moments in jazz

Aug. 11, 1957: Tito Puente loses the beat

Nov. 3, 1963: Ella Fitzgerald hits a flat note

Sept. 9, 1948: Dizzy Gillespie can't find Bb

July 14, 1974: Oscar Peterson forgets the chords to "Heart and Soul."

"Well, thank God we all made it out in time.
... 'Course, now we're equally screwed."

"Hey, Bob...did I scare you or what?"

48

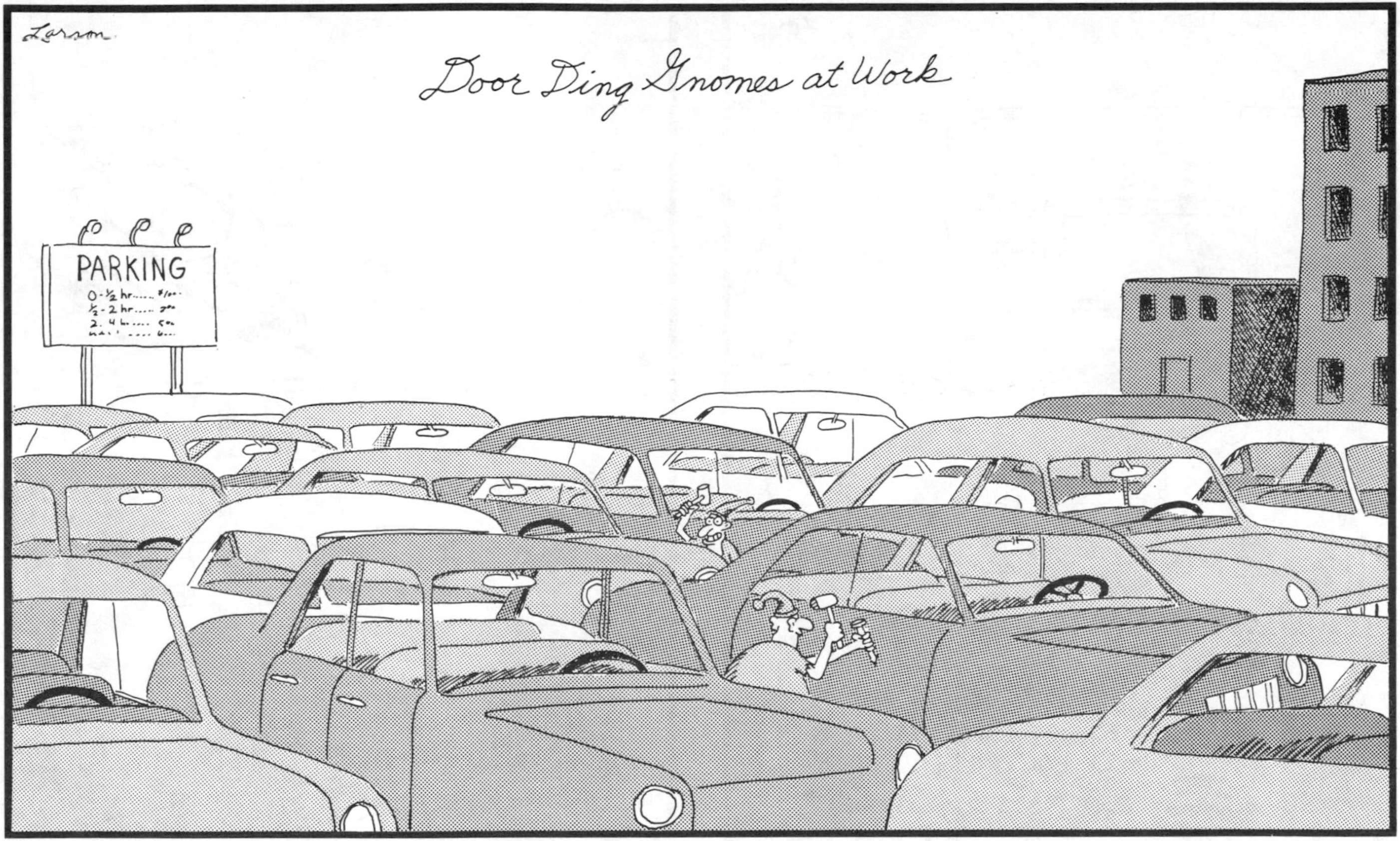
Larson
PARKING
Door Ding Gnomes at Work

"Bobby, jiggle Grandpa's rat so it looks alive, please."

"So…they tell me you're pretty handy with a gun."

Mountain families

Hummingbirds on vacation

Fruitcakes of the World

Butterfly yearbooks

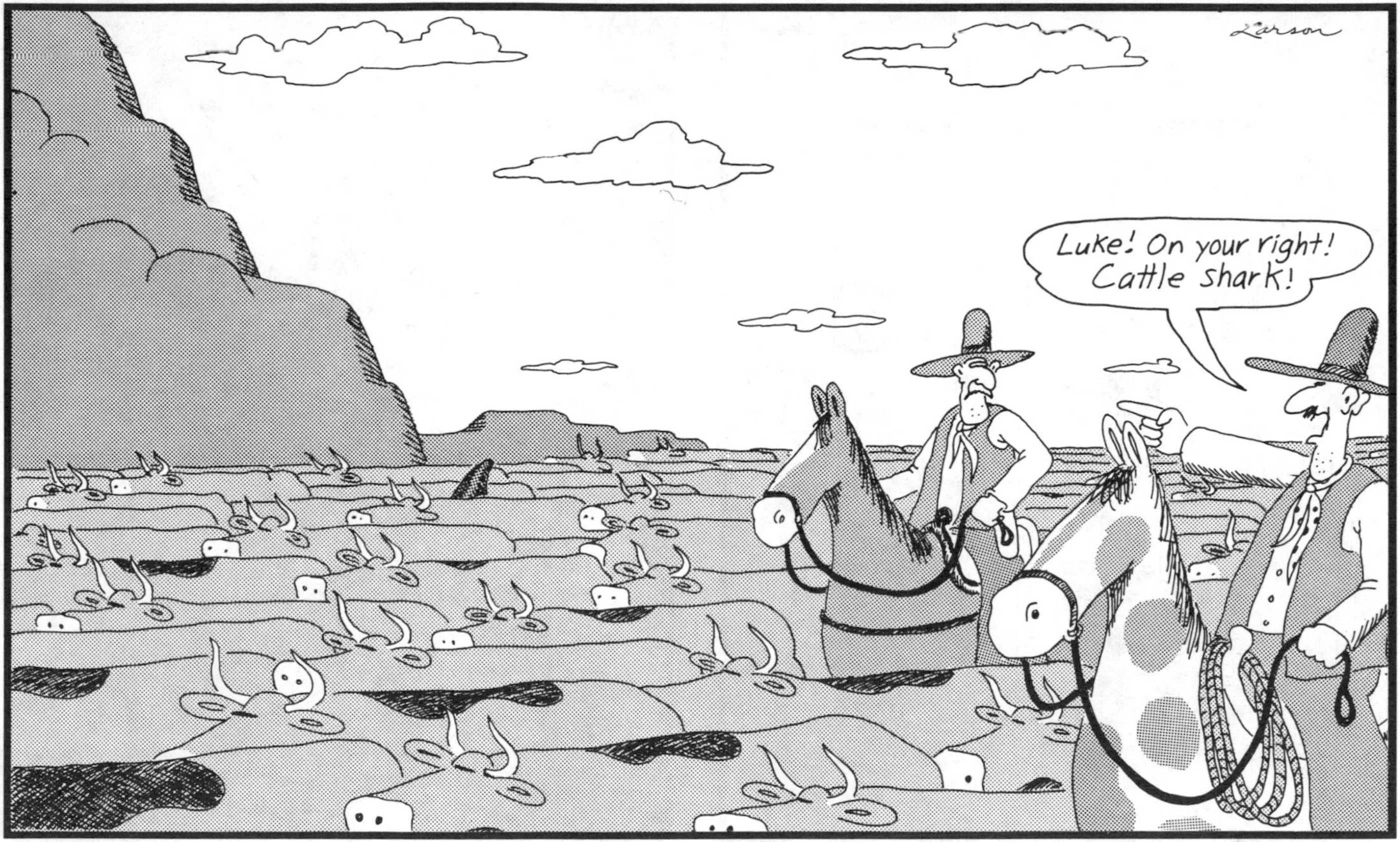
Larson
Luke! On your right! Cattle shark!

"Oh, for heaven's sake, Miss Carlisle! ...
They're only cartoon animals!"

Primitive think tanks

Fly travelogues

Her answer off by miles, Sheila's "cow sense" was always a target of ridicule.

55

The famous "Mr. Ed vs. Francis the Talking Mule" debates

Scene from *Bring 'Em Back Preserved*

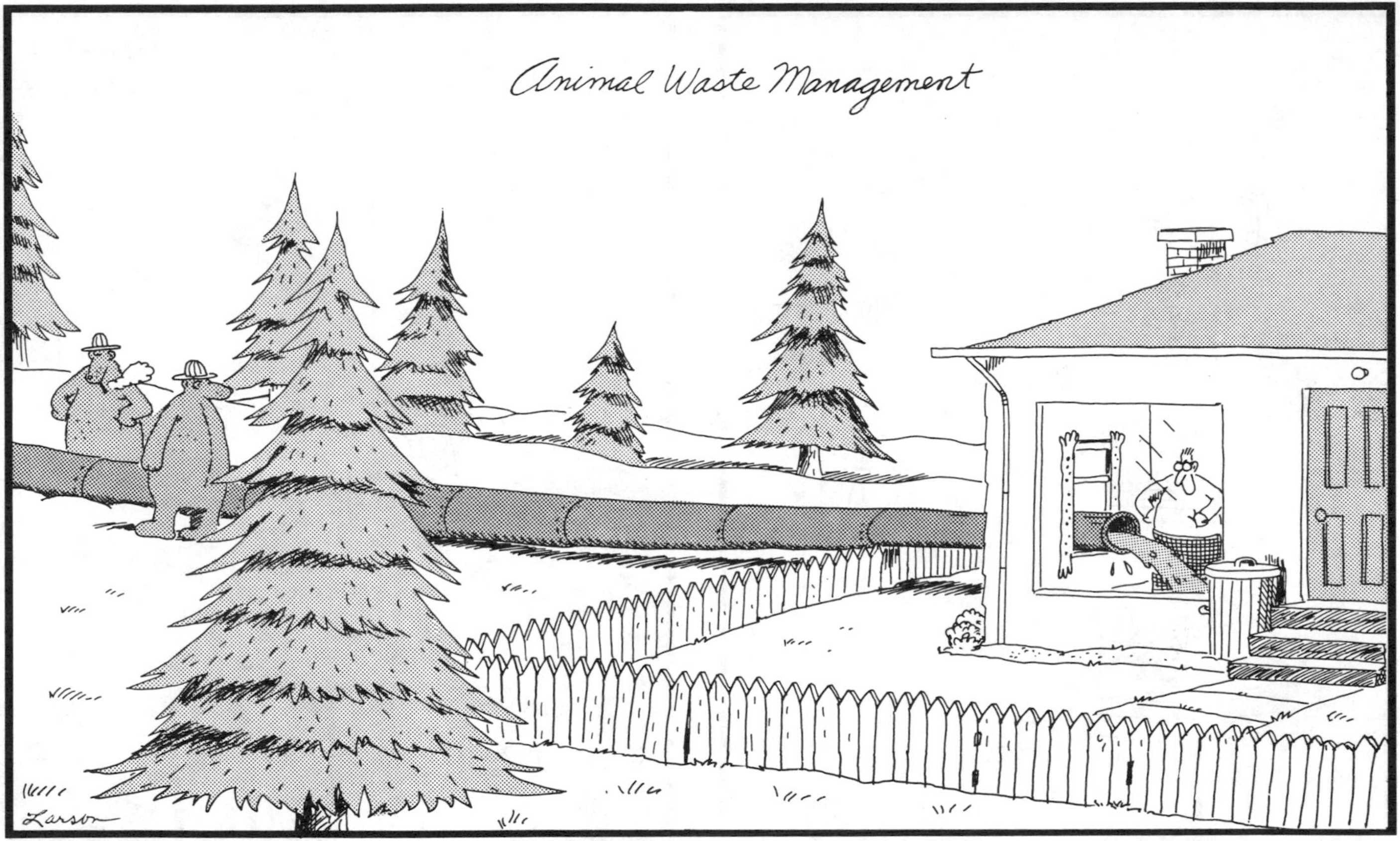
Animal Waste Management
Larson

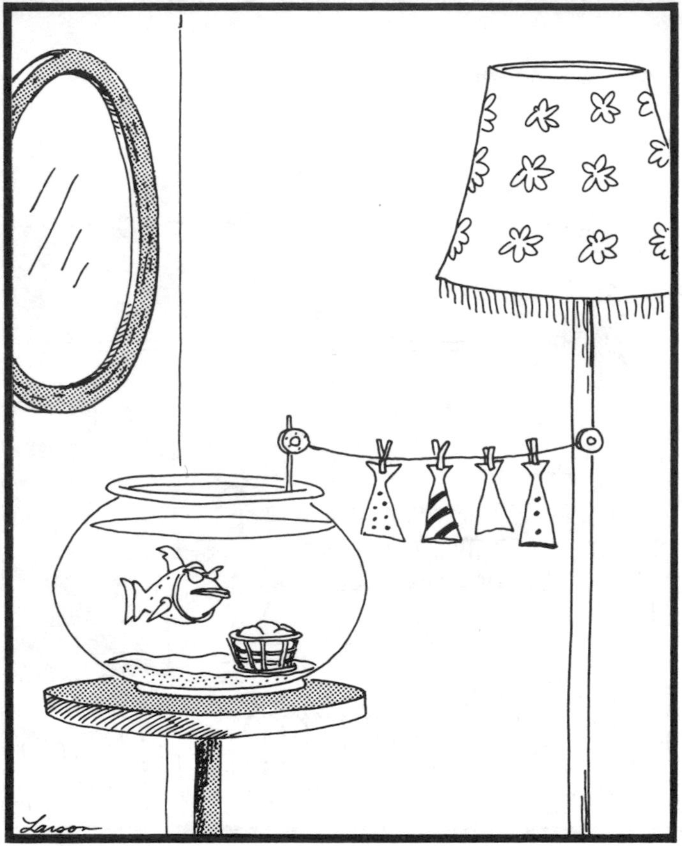
Larson

Goldfish laundry days

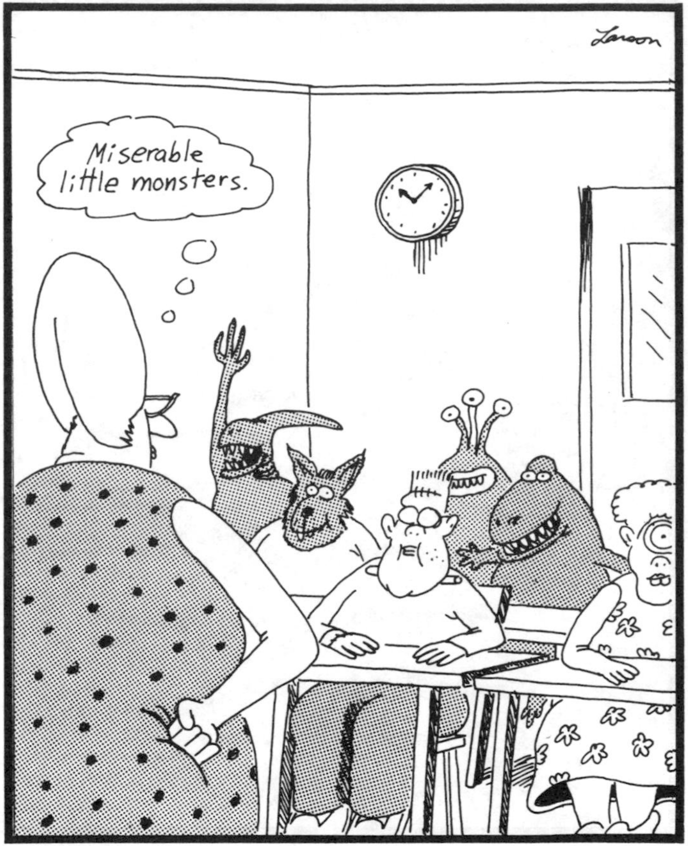
Larson
Miserable little monsters.

"Yeah, yeah, buddy, I've heard it all before: You've just metamorphosed and you've got 24 hours to find a mate and breed before you die. ... Well, get lost!"

"All right! Hand me the tongs, Frank. ... We got us a big den of rattlers here."

59

Aladdin's lamp, end table, and sofa

Monster jobs

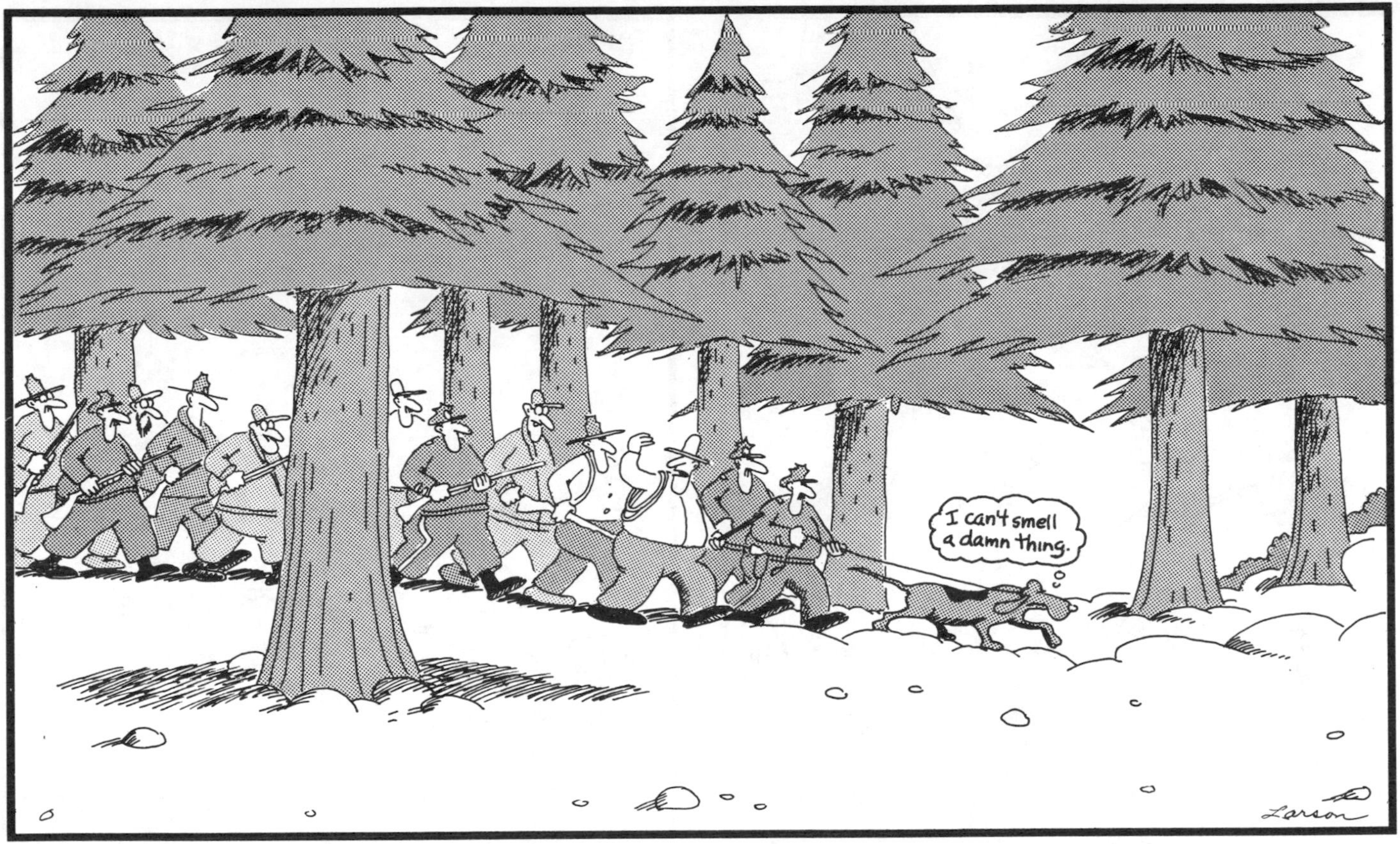
I can't smell a damn thing.
Larson

"You and Fred have such a lovely web, Edna —
and I *love* what you've done with those fly wings."

Professor Feldman, traveling back in time, gradually succumbs to the early stages of nonculture shock.

"The wench, you idiot! Bring me the *wench!*"

"Well, this may not be wise on a first date, but I just gotta try your garlic wharf rats."

The world was going down the tubes. They needed a scapegoat. They found Wayne.

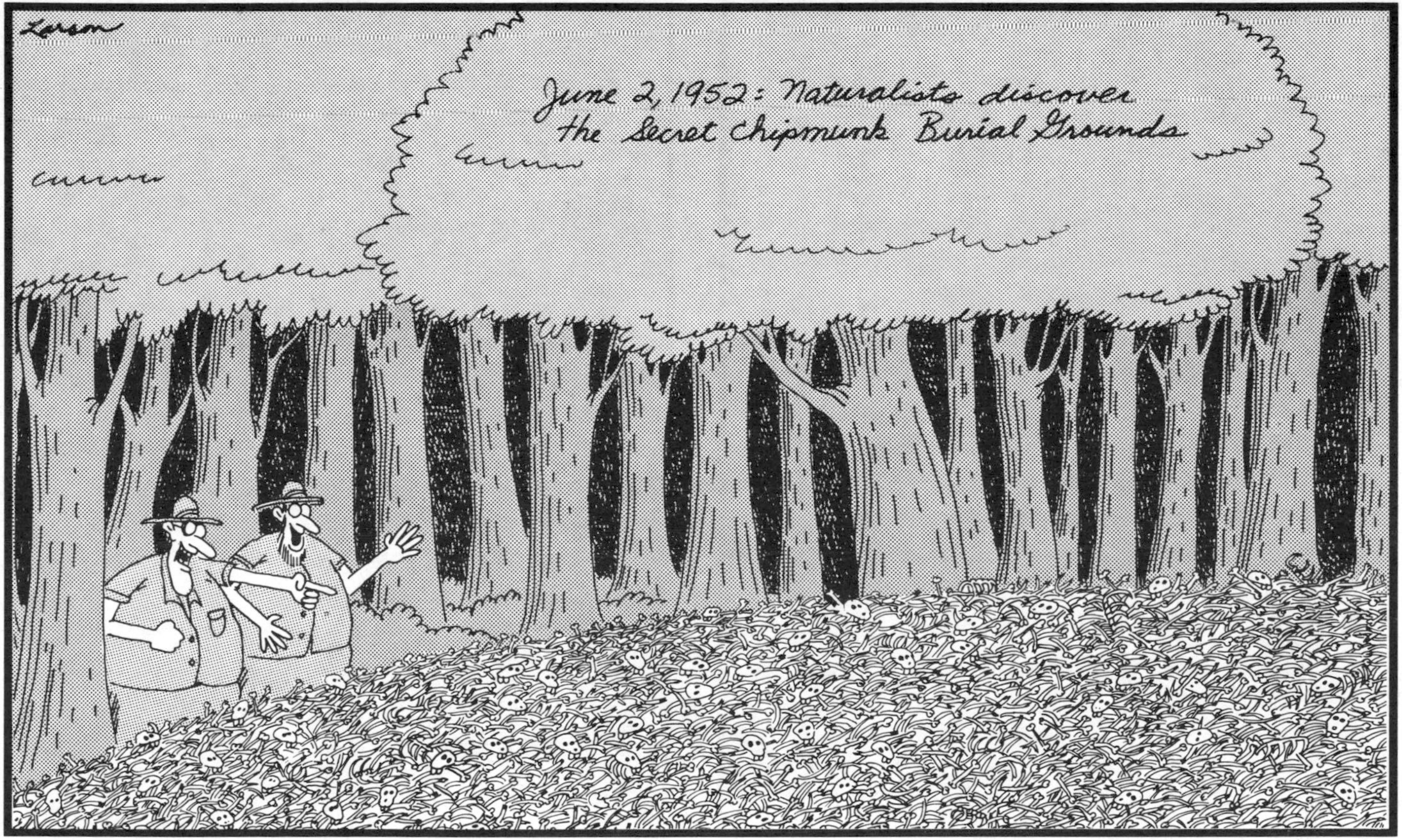
June 2, 1952: Naturalists discover the Secret Chipmunk Burial Grounds

"Well, the Sullivans are out on their tire again."

"Hold it! There's a car across the street — you sure you weren't followed, Mary?"

"Well! No wonder! ... Look who's been loose the whole evening!"

"And this report just in. ... Apparently, the grass *is* greener on the other side."

Cockroach nightmares

The toaster divers of Pago Pago

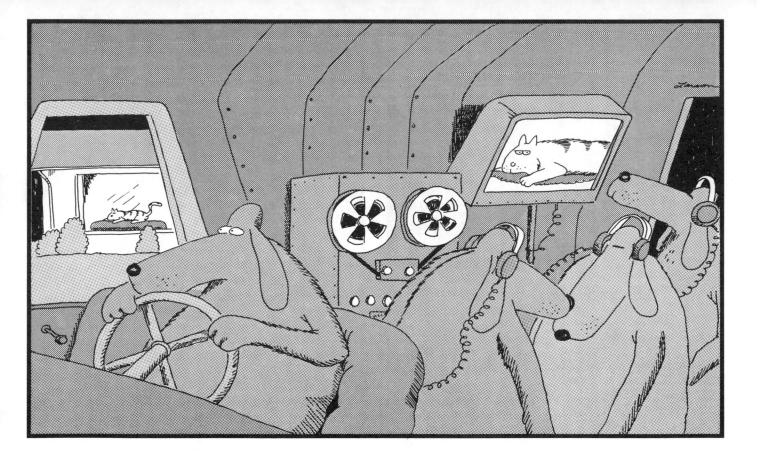

The untold ending of D.B. Cooper

BEN & VERA'S
ROTTWEILER
FARM

Robby works his ant farm.

"You want me to stop the car, Larry, or do you want to take your brother off the rack this instant?"

71

An instant later, both Professor Waxman and his time machine
are obliterated, leaving the cold-blooded/warm-blooded
dinosaur debate still unresolved.

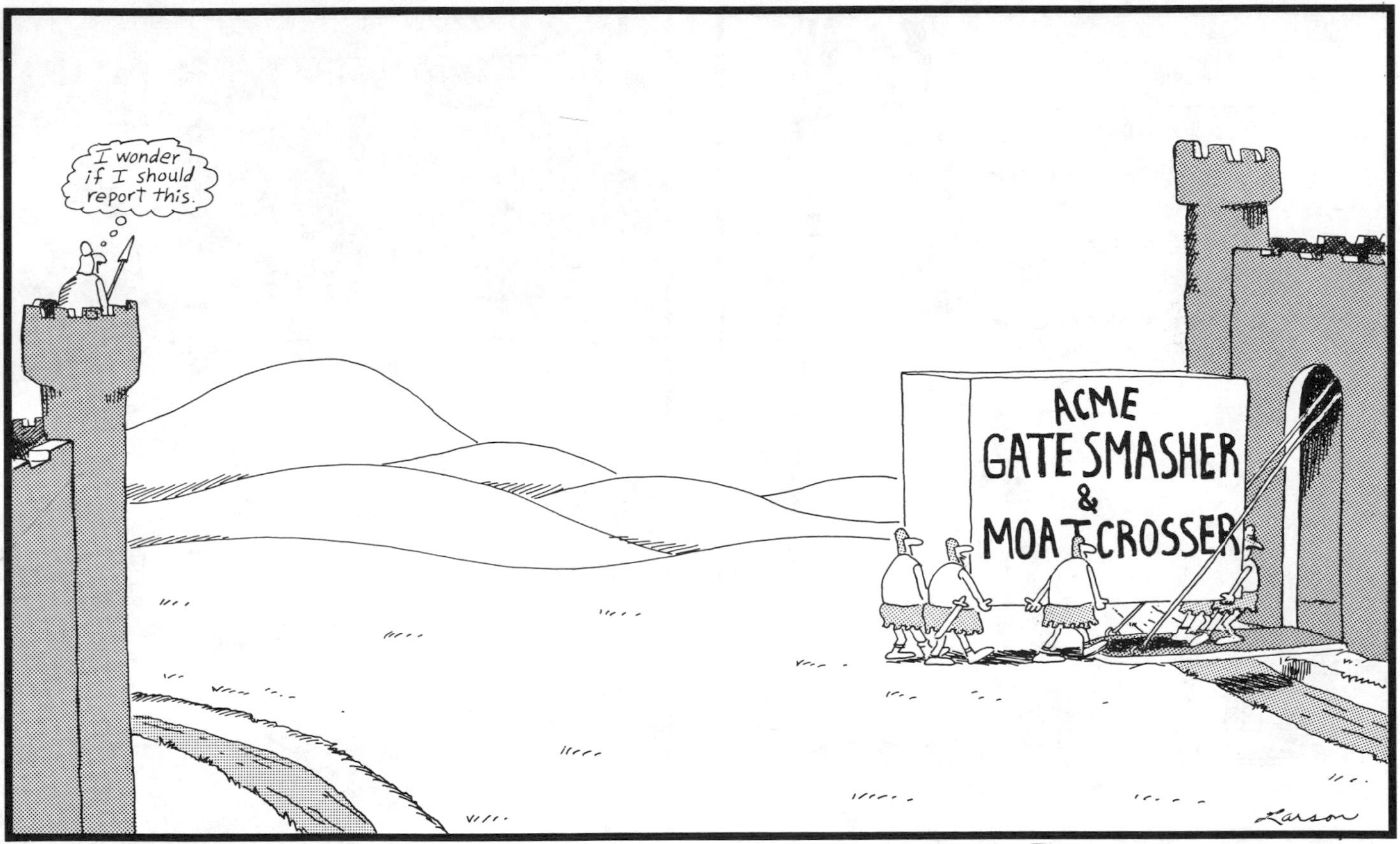
I wonder if I should report this.
ACME GATE SMASHER & MOAT CROSSER
Larson

Michelangelo's father

Saloon scenes on other planets

Full moon and empty head

"Now relax. ... Just like last week, I'm going to hold the cape up for the count of 10. ... When you start getting angry, I'll put it down."

75

Edgar Allan Poe in a moment of writer's block

The elephant man meets a buffalo gal.

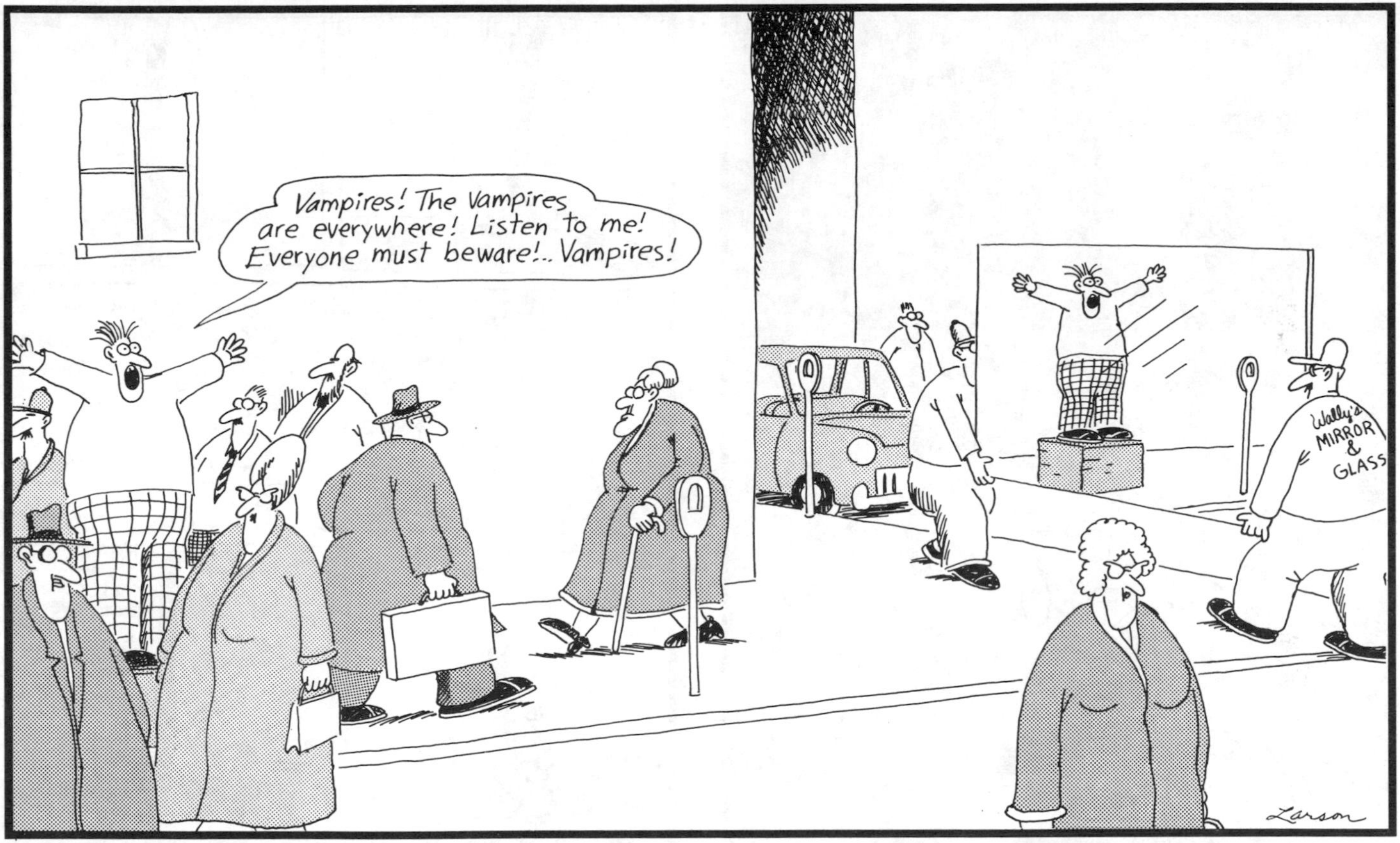
Vampires! The Vampires are everywhere! Listen to me! Everyone must beware!.. Vampires!
Wally's MIRROR & GLASS
Larson

The big-lipped dogs of the equatorial rain forest

78

Young Victor Frankenstein stays after school.

"Let go, Morty! Let go, Morty! You're pulling me in!
... Let go, Morty! You're pulling me in!"

"Well, it's cold again."

Humpty's final resting place.

"What the? ... This is lemonade! Where's my culture of amoebic dysentery?"

"Man, this is havin' no effect. ... But if the boss wants this varmint dragged through the desert, I ain't gonna argue."

"Well, well — another blond hair. ... Conducting a little more 'research' with that Jane Goodall tramp?"

"Not bad, but you guys wanna see a *really* small horse?"

"No, no, no! What are you doing? ... Fifth leg! Fifth leg!"

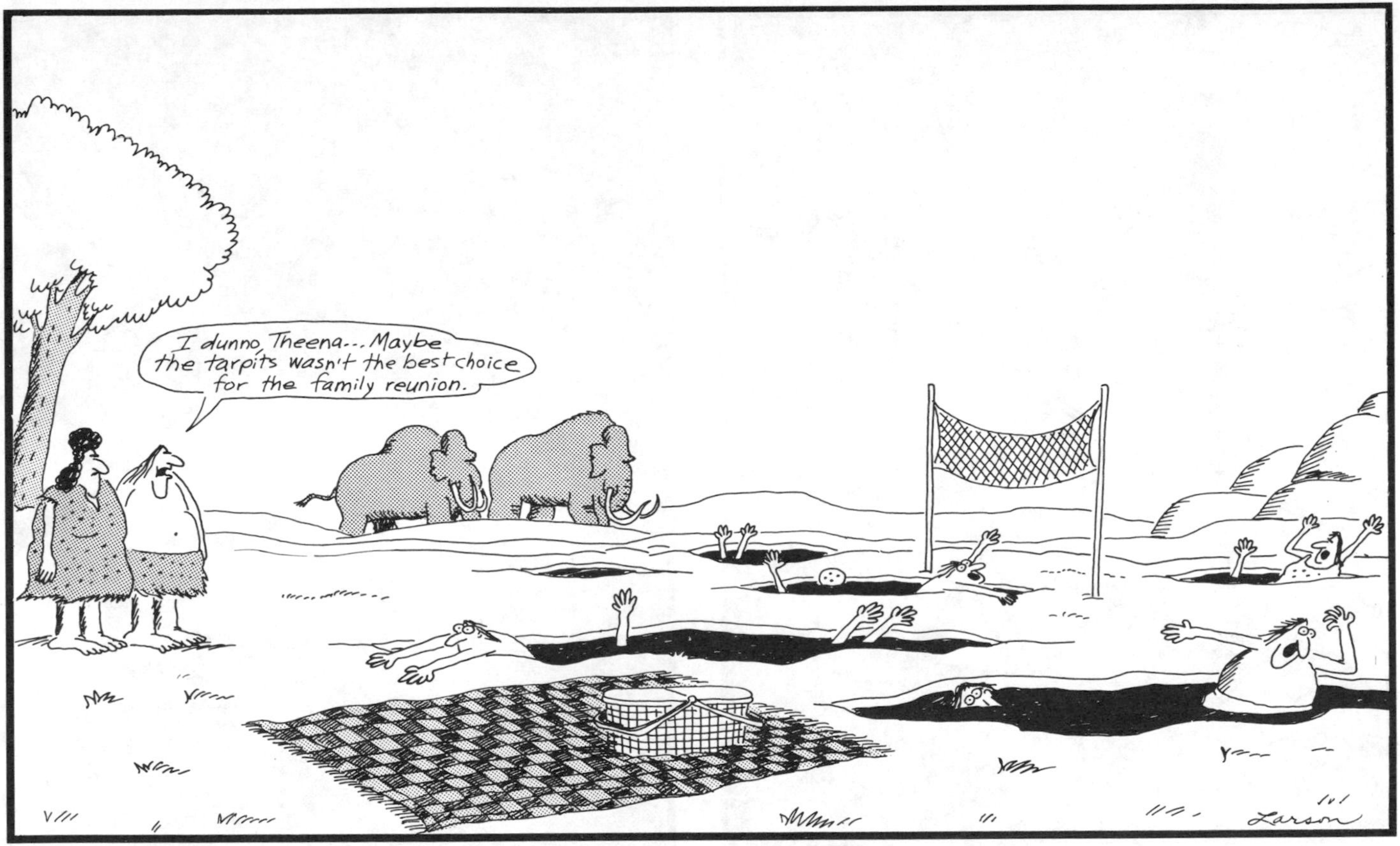
I dunno, Theena... Maybe the tarpits wasn't the best choice for the family reunion.
Larson

"That does it, Sid. ... You yell 'tarantula' one more time and
you're gonna be wearin' this thing."

And by coincidence, Carl had just reached the "m's."

Early archaeologists

Crossing paths on their respective
journeys of destiny, Johnny Appleseed and
Irving Ragweed nod "hello."

Roger crams for his microbiology midterm.

"Tell it again, Gramps! The one about being caught in the shark frenzy off the Great Barrier Reef!"

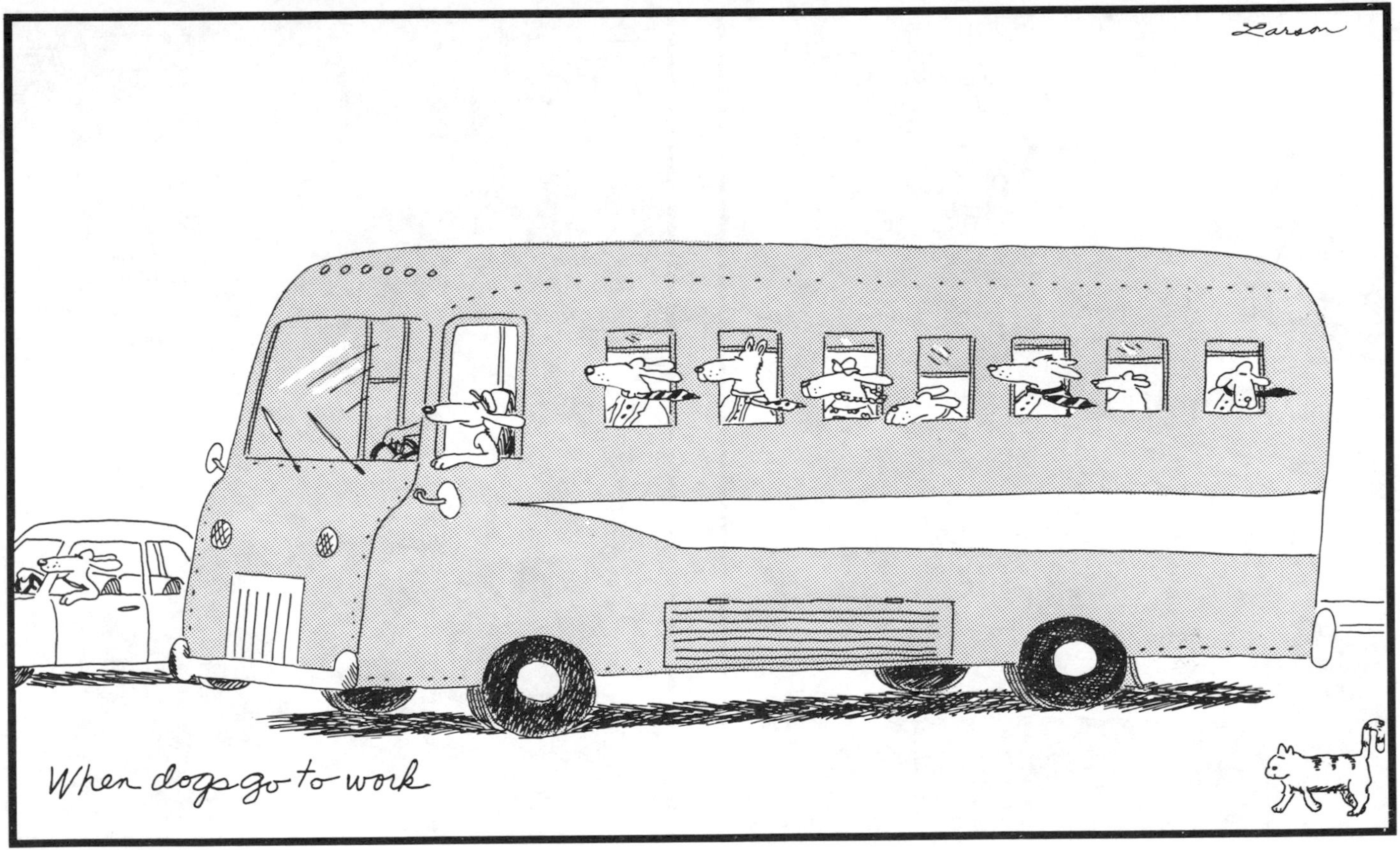
Larson

When dogs go to work

Accountant street gangs

Just when you thought it was safe to go back into the topsoil.

The fake McCoys

"Zelda! Cool it! ... The Rothenbergs hear the can opener!"

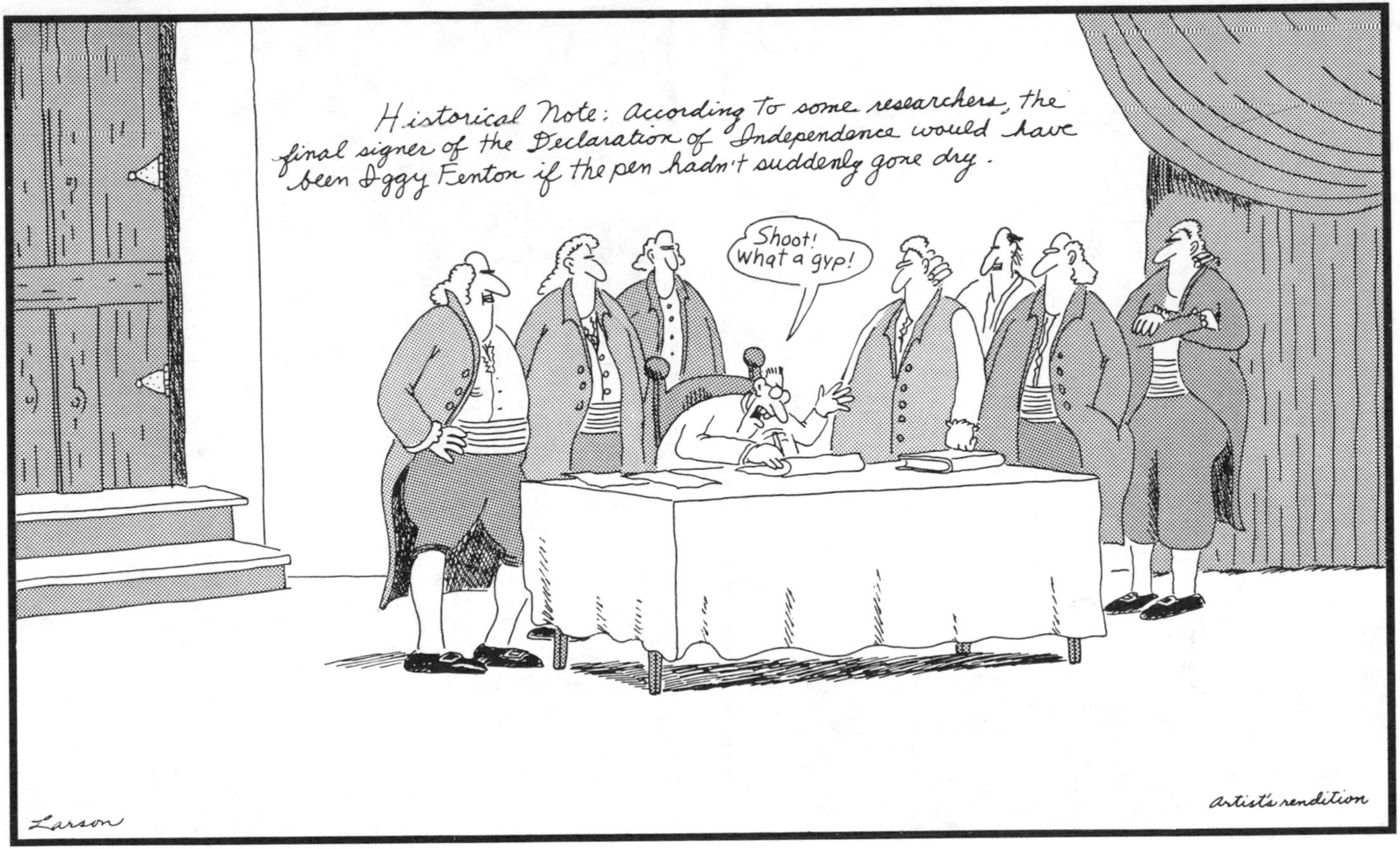
Historical Note: According to some researchers, the final signer of the Declaration of Independence would have been Iggy Fenton if the pen hadn't suddenly gone dry.
Shoot! What a gyp!
Larson
artist's rendition

Inexplicably, Bob's porcupine goes flat.

"Carl, maybe you should just leave your flashlight off. We're trying to scare these kids, not crack 'em up."

Killer bees are generally described
as starting out as larvae delinquents.

The spitting cobras at home

Thor's hammer, screwdriver, and crescent wrench

"I had them all removed last week and, boy, do I feel great."

Early piñatas

"Hey, everyone! Simmons here just uttered a discouraging word!"

"Letter from Lonso. ...And he sounds pretty lonely."

"Man, Ben, I'm gettin' tired of this. ...How many days now we've been eatin' this trail dust?"

Although skilled with their pillow arsenal, the Wimpodites were favorite targets of Viking attacks

Larson

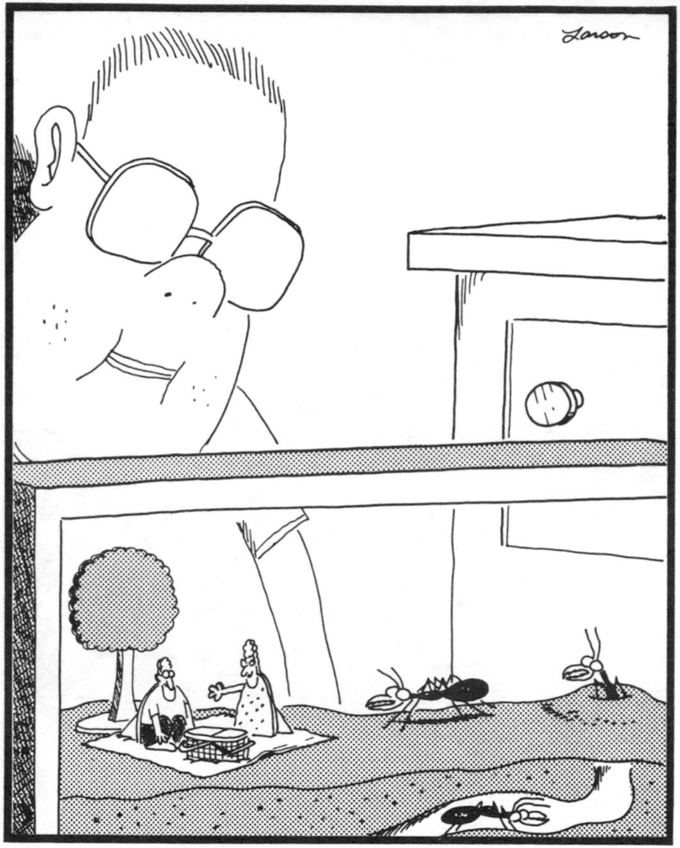
Larson

Stephen King's childhood ant farm

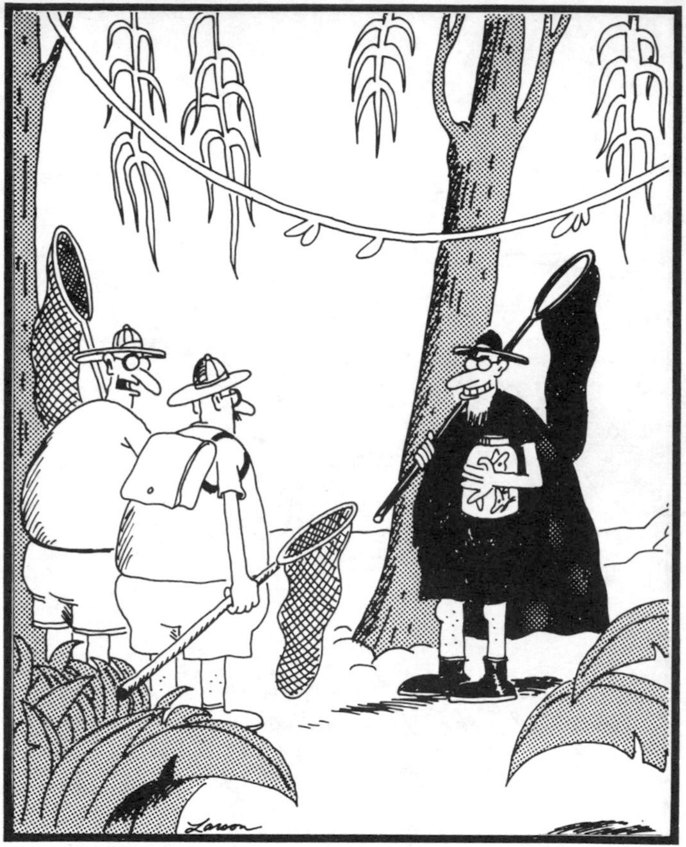
Larson

"Egad! It's Professor DeArmond — the epitome of evil amongst butterfly collectors!"

Trick clubbing exhibitions

"Well, look who's excited to see you back
from being declawed."

"Aaaaaaaaaaaaaa! Earl! ...
We've got a poultrygeist!"

"Mom! ... Earl's grossing me out with a mouthful of worms!"

At the hospital for mothers whose children stepped on sidewalk cracks

At the Old Cartoonists' Home